THE GUIDANCE OF THE HOLY SPIRIT

THE GUIDANCE OF THE HOLY SPIRIT

by Annette Capps

Unless otherwise indicated, all Scripture quotations are taken from the *New Living Translation.*

27 26 25 03 02 01

The Guidance of the Holy Spirit
ISBN-13: 978-1-937578-81-7

Published by Capps Publishing
P.O. Box 10
Broken Arrow, Oklahoma 74013

CONTENTS

CONTENTS

CHAPTER 1

The Holy Spirit

Jesus said in John 16:13, "*When the Spirit of truth comes, he will guide you into all truth. He will not speak on his own but will tell you what he has heard. He will tell you about the future.*"

The disciples were dependent on Jesus to help them understand spiritual truths as well as everyday life. When Jesus left, they required help, just as we do. The Holy Spirit came to dwell with them and in them to give them understanding and access to all the wisdom of God.

"He is the Holy Spirit, who leads into all truth. The world cannot receive him, because it isn't looking for him and doesn't recognize him. But you know him, because he lives with you now and later will be in you" (John 14:17).

All the treasures of wisdom and knowledge are in the person of the Holy Spirit and He dwells within us! Paying attention to our inward witness (some call this intuition) can prevent tragedy in our lives and loved ones. The Holy Spirit bears witness with our spirit and through that inner knowing we can follow His guidance.

CHAPTER 2

4 Ways We Can Be Guided by the Holy Spirit

Each person is unique and the guidance we receive is unique to us. Let's look at four of the ways that we perceive the guidance of the Holy Spirit:

1. Knowing
2. Seeing (Vision)
3. Hearing (Auditory)
4. Feeling (Kinesthetic)

Knowing, or an inward witness, is one of the most difficult to describe because knowledge is simply a concept. It is not physical, nor can you really physically describe it. When you "know" something, you just know it. Many times I have had this "knowing" about certain people. I've either known they were of a good spirit, or sometimes I've just known they were not to be trusted, something was amiss. How do you explain that? The Holy Spirit certainly knows all things, but I did not hear a voice or have a vision. I did not seek an "answer;" rather this was just an instantaneous knowledge that was transmitted and I received it.

My personal opinion is that people carry their "stuff" with them all the time. Their "stuff" could be all the decisions they have made, all the acts they have committed, their beliefs, thoughts, and motives. They wear these like clothes. Sometimes this "stuff" appears in their physical features. Have you ever looked at someone and thought, "Boy, have they had a hard life!" You could see it on their face.

The Holy Spirit and God's Word Make Changes

The power of the Holy Spirit and God's Word can make changes in someone from the inside out. I have met Christians who lived horrible lives in the past, but you can't see it or know it because they have totally let go of the past. It is no longer with them.

The real challenge with "knowing" is to remain nonjudgmental even when you "know" things. Knowing will help protect you and guide you to make the right decisions, but it is not helpful to use that knowledge to judge another person's life. Just observe and move on.

Also be aware that what a person carries with them right now could be different a year from now depending on their spiritual growth and ability to let go of old beliefs, motives and thought processes. Part of the "stuff" we carry with us that is perceptible to everyone's "knower" are intangible beliefs and thoughts. When a person carries a "victim mentality," others perceive this, especially perpetrators who victimize others. That is one of the reasons that the cycles repeat themselves.

Through knowing or sensing what is surrounding another person, we can avoid many pitfalls and not become involved with the wrong person.

CHAPTER 3

Knowing About Situations

Many years ago, my ministry was growing and the employees were in need of more space for work and filling orders. There was a church in town that we were all associated with and had held meetings there, as well as being friends with the lady who was the pastor. The church needed to move out of the building but there was a year left on the lease. I suggested that my ministry could sublease the building, relieving them of their commitment and giving us more space. Everyone was thrilled with this prospect, however, when it was time to sign the papers, I suddenly had a very unsettling feeling about the process. It felt like a large, heavy rock was in my stomach. I couldn't get past it, so I backed out of the deal. Later I found out that there were liens and outstanding debts that I would have been obligated to pay if I had signed those papers. Thank God for the warning!

Situations Will Present Themselves

Sometimes situations will present themselves in your life that look good, sound good, and feel good. But somewhere in the process things change and you no longer have peace about it. When this happens, STOP. Either you don't have enough information, the timing is wrong, or something has changed. It is a mistake to think that if you have a leading about a situation, you can jump right in. In every part of the process, it is imperative to listen for the Holy Spirit.

You could know that it would be good for you to refinance your house, but after completing the application, you don't feel quite the same. Slow down and see what is going on. Is it the right timing? What if you waited 3–4 weeks and the interest rates went down? Is this the mortgage company that is right for you? You may delay for a week and find out you have been promoted on your job, which entails a relocation. Often the Holy Spirit will give you the answer before you even know the question! Something is missing or something is not quite right. That doesn't mean that your "knower" didn't work; it just means that things will work out in a different way than you thought. A negative knowing is just as valuable as a positive knowing. If you don't feel exactly right, don't do it!

CHAPTER 4

Averting Tragedy

John 16:13 tells us that the Holy Spirit will tell us or show us things to come. I am convinced He always tries to warn us of things ahead of time if we will listen. I was teaching in a convention in California when I had a sudden urgent feeling that someone in my family was in danger. I excused myself from the dinner table and went to the hotel room and began to pray in the Spirit. It was then that I knew I was praying for my sister

Beverly and her children. I asked for the Holy Spirit and the angels to intervene for her protection. When I called, I found out that as my sister was traveling in Arkansas, her car narrowly avoided a fatal accident at that exact time.

Bad Feeling About Going On Vacation

One of the ways that I know the difference between ordinary fear and an impression of the Holy Spirit to pray for protection is that it is totally unexpected. If you are watching the evening news about terrorism and start having a bad feeling about going on vacation, then it's hard to decipher whether you are worried because of the negative news report or the Holy Spirit is trying to warn you.

Staying neutral is the best place for being able to tell the difference. Don't saturate yourself with negativity in any form. If you are loaded down with negative thoughts and feelings all the time, how can you know when you are "checked" in your spirit, or receive a warning? By staying neutral, peaceful in your life, you are more open to the leadings of the Spirit.

When you have a leading to proceed in any matter, get as much information as you can. The information may or may not affect your final decision, but it may allow you to clear out problems before they grow to an unmanageable size. When I attempted to sublease that church building, I was faced with paying off debts I did not incur. If I had checked this out thoroughly, I would have obtained that information.

Instead, I went on the positive feeling that was being generated. (I think this positive feeling was the pastor and employees' relief and excitement that I felt.) Fortunately, even in my ignorance, the Holy Spirit got through to me. I almost overrode that because I did not want to disappoint everyone. That would have been a high price to pay to make others happy!

In the book of Acts, chapter 9, verse 11, the Lord appeared to Ananias in a vision and spoke to him to go lay his hands on Saul that he might receive his sight. This was both a visual and an auditory experience for Ananias. When you look at the circumstances (Saul was persecuting Christians), it would take a very strong impression of some sort to convince Ananias to go pray for Saul. He could have been killed!

CHAPTER 5

Seeing in the Spirit

The most common experience among Christians is to be led by a "knowing" (or a witness to their spirit); however there are times when people perceive things by "seeing." Those who perceive guidance visually use terms such as "I saw in my spirit . . ." or "I just saw what God wanted me to do."

Now in everyday life, you generally don't need a strong vision from God about how to proceed with your daily life. You can just follow the subtle guidance and direction in your spirit. However, if you have a vision or an angel appears to you, then it must really be important! There are times when I have what I call "mini-visions." I am not in a trance but perfectly alert when suddenly a scene passes through my mind. This scene is not visible to the physical eye, but through my "mind's eye." Because of this "scene," I become aware of facts about a situation that I had not known before. Or, I know that I am supposed to go to this certain place.

Many years ago, I was driving down the street, minding my own business, when a vision appeared to me. I saw myself walking into the room of a hospital in Tulsa and laying hands on a woman I knew. She jumped out of bed healed of severe back problems. Along with this vision, I felt a very obvious anointing of healing. This vision was so strong that I drove straight to the hospital, asked for the woman's room, walked in and did exactly what I saw in my vision. Now, I did not tell her anything about the vision until later, but she jumped out of bed and danced around the room, praising God with her hands raised in the air exactly as I saw in the vision. It was such a remarkable healing that the nurse ran into the corridor calling out, "There has been a healing in room 2812! Someone get the doctor!"

Seeing a Vision, *Feeling* an Anointing, and *Knowing*

This incident combined *seeing* a vision, *feeling* an anointing, and *knowing* what I should do. Although this was a very powerful experience, these modalities of guidance happen often to me in a much subtler way. I will have a "flash" of something I need to attend to now, or the picture of a person's face will come before me and I know I should contact them.

To those people who are more inclined to register things in an auditory manner, guidance is perceived by them as "hearing something." The hearing doesn't actually happen with the ear itself, but is expressed as "I heard in my spirit" or "I heard it in my heart."

CHAPTER 6

Developing Discernment

It is of the utmost importance that you exercise discernment in following any form of guidance. There have been Christians who follow after visions, voices, and prophesies because they seemed supernatural. They left a trail of destruction behind them because they did not test the spirits to see if they are of God. One of the biggest mistakes that Christians make is "seeking guidance." When a person gets desperate for guidance or the answer to a question, there are always voices that will rush into that void and fill it with something. The safest guidance is from *within you.*

It is best to have an open mind and heart so that the Holy Spirit can choose what method He uses to lead you. A good prayer would be, *"Holy Spirit, I ask for your direction and guidance so that I may live in God's perfect will for my life. I open myself to Your guidance because you dwell in me."* The Holy Spirit never forces anything, but gently directs and guides with joy. If the guidance you receive does not bring peace, joy, or confirmation, then it is to be examined very carefully or cast off.

If I don't have peace or know what I am supposed to do about something, I wait. Doing nothing can be a real challenge, but if you don't have the answer, it can be foolish to jump into a decision. When being pressed for a yes or no answer to a commitment, I have found that it is best to decline rather than agree to something that I don't have peace about.

CHAPTER 7

Pay Attention

In developing discernment, always pay attention to your first impressions. If you feel uncomfortable, anxious, or pressured, then be aware that things may not be as they appear. I have known people who have attended meetings because everyone else gave wonderful reports. Later, great deception was exposed and I asked these people if they had any check in their spirit warning them that something was wrong. Their reply was very alarming, "Yes, I did not feel just right at first, but everyone else thought it was great. There were healings, so I thought it was just me."

Always trust the Holy Spirit inside of you and proceed with caution if "things don't seem just right." All external experiences should be checked and compared with the Word and the witness of your spirit. God has given us supernatural protection, a guide into the truth, if we only listen. Pay attention!

CHAPTER 8

Led by the Word of God

So what if I don't feel like I am being led of the Spirit? Your primary source of hearing from God has already been given to you in printed form, the Bible. The Spirit of God will speak to your heart through the written Word. He anoints the words and they seem to jump off the page just for you.

God speaks to me and guides me every day through the scriptures. All we have to do is pick up the Bible and start reading. One of my favorite scriptures is Proverbs 6:22 AMPC, and I make it into a personal declaration of faith:

"When I go, the Word of God *leads* me, when I sleep, it *keeps* me, when I wake, it *talks* with me."

There have been times when I needed direction and scriptures started popping into my mind. When seeking God for answers, I was led to read just the right passage or story that brought clarity. When you are reading the Word, you are absorbing divinely inspired words that are alive, active, and energizing to your soul. Follow the light of the Word; it is a lamp to light your way!

PRAYER OF SALVATION

God loves you — no matter who you are, no matter what your past. God loves you so much that He gave His one and only begotten Son for you. The Bible tells us that *"...whoever believes in him shall not perish but have eternal life"* (John 3:16 NIV). Jesus laid down His life and rose again so that we could spend eternity with Him in heaven and experience His absolute best on earth. If you would like to receive Jesus into your life, pray the following prayer out loud and mean it from your heart.

Heavenly Father, I come to You admitting that I am a sinner. Right now, I choose to turn away from sin, and I ask You to cleanse me of all unrighteousness. I believe that Your Son, Jesus, died on the cross to take away my sins. I also believe that He rose again from the dead so that I might be forgiven of my sins and made righteous through faith in Him. I call upon the name of Jesus Christ and confess Him to be the Savior and Lord of my life. Jesus, I choose to follow You and ask that You fill me with the power of the Holy Spirit. I declare that right now I am a child of God. I am free from sin and full of the righteousness of God. I am saved in Jesus' name. Amen.

For a complete list of CDs, DVDs, and books by Capps Ministries, write:

Capps Ministries

P.O. Box 10, Broken Arrow, Oklahoma 74013

501-842-2576

E-Books & MP3's Available

cappsministries.com

Visit us online for:

Radio Broadcasts in Your Area

Concepts of Faith Television

Broadcast listings:

Local Stations, **Daystar,**

The VICTORY Channel,

& **TCT Network**

youtube.com/CappsMinistries

facebook.com/CharlesCappsMinistries

BOOKS BY CHARLES CAPPS AND ANNETTE CAPPS

30-Day Devotional

Shaping Tomorrow:

How Today's Words Frame Your Future

Angels

*God's Creative Power® for Finances**

*God's Creative Power® – Gift Edition**

(Now Available — Hardback Edition, Vegan Leather Gift Edition, and Spanish Paperback)

BOOKS BY ANNETTE CAPPS

The Spirit of Prophecy

Overcoming Persecution

Reverse the Curse in Your Body and Emotions

*Quantum Faith®**

Removing the Roadblocks to Health and Healing

The Guidance of the Holy Spirit

*Also Available in Spanish

BOOKS BY CHARLES CAPPS

Calling Things That Are Not

Triumph Over the Enemy

When Jesus Prays Through You

The Tongue – A Creative Force

(Now Available—Hardback Edition)

Releasing the Ability of God Through Prayer

End Time Events

Authority in Three Worlds

Changing the Seen and Shaping the Unseen

Faith That Will Not Change

Faith and Confession

*God's Creative Power® Will Work for You**

*God's Creative Power® for Healing**

Success Motivation Through the Word

God's Image of You

*Seedtime and Harvest**

*The Thermostat of Hope**

How You Can Avoid Tragedy

Kicking Over Sacred Cows

The Substance of Things

The Light of Life in the Spirit of Man

Faith That Will Work for You

*Also Available in Spanish

BOOKS BY CHARLES CAPPS

[illegible] Things That Are Not

[illegible]

[illegible]

[illegible]

[illegible]

[illegible]

[illegible]

[illegible]

Faith and [illegible]

Faith and Confession

God's Creative Power Will Work for You

[illegible]

[illegible]

[illegible]

[illegible]

[illegible]

[illegible]

[illegible]

[illegible]

[illegible]

[illegible]

SHAPING TOMORROW

How Today's Words Frame Your Future

By Charles Capps with Annette Capps

Creating the Blueprints for Your Future

The words you speak today are shaping your tomorrow!

This 30-day devotional book takes you on a faith journey through the powerful, scriptural principles that changed Charles Capps and his family forever. With his personal stories, practical applications, and down-to-earth humor, you will learn how to apply these powerful Bible principles to your own life:

- The Power of Your Words
- Calling for What You Want
- Creating a New Image Inside of You
- Developing Supernatural Hope

"The words you speak are the seeds you are planting in your heart. Speak the promise until it becomes your reality." — Charles Capps

A Portal to the Presence and Power of God

The Spirit of Prophecy

by Annette Capps

Annette shares her own supernatural encounters with the Holy Spirit and His gifts. She offers unique insight into the seemingly contradictory prophecies being given today and in the past. Also included, prophecies delivered by Charles Capps that are still speaking power and revelation to the body of Christ.

You are living in the Last Days. It's time to step into the prophetic anointing that ushers in the end-time harvest.

Your Curse Has Already Been Reversed

Reverse the Curse

In Your Body and Emotions

There are many wounded and brokenhearted people in the Body of Christ who are suffering in their mind and emotions. The battleground of Satan's attack has been in the mental arena. Yet there has not been any practical teaching that would guide people into mental and emotional wholeness.

This book will show you how to reverse the emotional curse and in so doing open the door for physical healing and miracles in believers' lives.

Doctors cannot reverse the curse of sickness. Only Jesus can reverse the curse and bring perfect healing and wholeness to an individual's life. Learn how to activate God's power in your body by speaking and acting your faith upon God's Word.

Annette Capps is the President and CEO of Capps Ministries, an ordained minister, businesswoman, and licensed airplane pilot. Her diverse experiences have shaped her unique and practical approach to ministry. Combining the supernatural with the natural, her balanced message of the practical and the prophetic stirs faith in the hearts of audiences.

A lifelong student of the Bible, Annette has ministered across the nation and authored several books, including *The Spirit of Prophecy* and her bestseller *Quantum Faith*®. In addition to continuing the radio ministry of her father, Charles Capps, Annette hosts the *Concepts of Faith* television program, which airs on many independent stations and networks, including Daystar, TCT Network, and The Victory Channel.

In 2025, Annette launched *Capps Chapel Radio* on the Oasis Radio Network. Every weekday, she shares prophetic insight, practical truths, and powerful teaching designed to strengthen and encourage listeners in their walk of faith. This 15-minute broadcast also streams live on the Oasis Radio Network app and at oasisnetwork.org.

Coming from a long family history of farming, Annette maintains a close connection with the land by managing her family's farmland in Arkansas and Oklahoma. She and her husband live in Broken Arrow, Oklahoma, where the ministry is now located.